Humorous
and
Nonsensical
poems

Liz Miles

Raintree

Raintree is an imprint of Capstone Global Library Limited, a company incorporated in England and Wales having its registered office at 7 Pilgrim Street, London, EC4V 6LB – Registered company number: 6695582

www.raintreepublishers.co.uk
myorders@raintreepublishers.co.uk

Text © Capstone Global Library Limited 2014
First published in hardback in 2014
The moral rights of the proprietor have been asserted.

Produced for Raintree by
White-Thomson Publishing
www.wtpub.co.uk
+44 (0)843 208 7460

Edited by Claudia Martin
Cover design by Tim Mayer
Designed by Ian Winton
Concept design by Alix Wood

Production by Victoria Fitzgerald
Originated by Capstone Global Library Ltd
Printed and bound in China

ISBN 978 1 4062 7291 8
17 16 15 14
10 9 8 7 6 5 4 3 2 1

British Library Cataloguing in Publication Data
A full catalogue record for this book is available from the British Library.

Poems reproduced by permission of:
p13, "A Jolly Young Fellow from Yuma", © 1967 by Ogden Nash, reprinted by permission of Curtis Brown, Ltd.
p 25, "Serious Luv" by Benjamin Zephaniah (Copyright © Benjamin Zephaniah) is reproduced by permission of United Agents (www.unitedagents.co.uk) on behalf of Benjamin Zephaniah.
p31, "Sick" from Where the Sidewalk Ends by Shel Silverstein. © 1974, renewed 2002 Evil Eye Music, LLC. Reprinted with permission from the Estate of Shel Silverstein, HarperCollins Children's Books, Edite Kroll Literary Agency Inc., and David Grossman Literary Agency.
p36, "Ice Cream War", © 2010 by Gary Soto, used by permission of the author.
p41, "Third and Last", from *Oh, Terrible Youth* © by Cristin O'Keefe Aptowicz (Write Bloody Publishing, 2011); www.aptowicz.com.
p47, "My Sister Turned into Barbie", © 2000 by Lindsay MacRae.

Picture credits can be found on page 63.

Every effort has been made to contact copyright holders of any material reproduced in this book. Any omissions will be rectified in subsequent printings if notice is given to the publisher.

Disclaimer
All the internet addresses (URLs) given in this book were valid at the time of going to press. However, due to the dynamic nature of the internet, some addresses may have changed, or sites may have changed or ceased to exist since publication. While the author and publisher regret any inconvenience this may cause readers, no responsibility for any such changes can be accepted by either the author or the publisher.

CONTENTS

Experiencing humorous and nonsensical poetry

Humorous poetry is poetry that makes you laugh or feel light-hearted and happy. It can make you chuckle or giggle, roll around on the floor roaring with laughter, or just smile.

What is it about **humorous** poetry that makes the reader laugh or smile? Some things are funny whether they are in a poem, a joke, a TV comedy, or a silly song:

- absurdity (e.g. a pink elephant riding across the sky on a banana)
- surprise (e.g. an ending to a story that you don't expect)
- exaggeration (e.g. a slug the size of a house)
- **puns** (e.g. broken pencils are pointless)
- slapstick (e.g. a custard tart in someone's face).

Poetic features

Poetry has its own forms and ways of getting humour across. In this book, we will explore how poets use poetic features for comedy and how they create light-hearted, humorous tones. For example, look out for these poetic tricks of the trade:

- Imagery – **imagery** is when the poet uses words to paint images or pictures that the reader can imagine
- Rhythm – there is a **rhythm** (beat) in all spoken words, and the poet plays with rhythm to stress humorous words, or to keep the poem moving in a lively, jolly way
- Rhyme – a **rhyme** scheme is how a poet places words that sound the same; this can emphasize funny words, and keep the tone lively
- Stanzas – poems are often split into **stanzas** (sets of lines); the breaks between the stanzas (where you usually pause when reading the poem) group the information logically and can also help make a poem funny.

What is nonsense poetry?

Nonsense poetry (or nonsensical poetry) is a type of **verse** that usually features wacky characters and their actions. It often involves unusual words – even words that have been made up and have no meaning!

Unlike some other humorous verse, nonsense poetry may not have a definite **theme** or message. For example, much of Lewis Carroll's poetry is dreamlike. In Carroll's 1865 novel *Alice's Adventures in Wonderland*, a character called the Hatter recites this poem:

> *Twinkle, twinkle, little bat!*
> *How I wonder what you're at!*
> *Up above the world you fly,*
> *Like a tea tray in the sky.*
> *Twinkle, twinkle, little bat!*
> *How I wonder what you're at!*

The verse is based on the well-known nursery rhyme "Twinkle, Twinkle, Little Star". So the word "bat" comes as a surprise. The image of a tea tray is nonsensical because a bat is nothing like a tea tray. While we can understand the poem, it has no logic. It is so nonsensical that it probably doesn't have a hidden message, other than: poems and words can be both confusing and fun!

The Hatter recites "Twinkle, Twinkle, Little Bat". A black and white version of this illustration by Sir John Tenniel (1820–1914) appeared in the first edition of *Alice's Adventures in Wonderland*.

What is the poem's purpose?

Poems, whether comic or not, often have a key idea or message to pass on to the reader. After reading a humorous poem, ask yourself: Is there more to this poem than funny images, a comic story, puns, or nonsense language?

What is the poem's audience?

Most of the poems in this book were written for children. But all the poems can be (and are) enjoyed by adults, too. Edward Lear's **limericks** (page 8) were written over 150 years ago, but are still admired today by people of all ages.

However, when reading the humorous poems in this book, it is important to think of the listener as well as the audience. Some poems are "spoken" by a character to an imaginary listener (for example, see "Sick" on page 31). If you imagine who the listener is meant to be, you can discover more about the meaning of the poem.

Some "performance poets", like the British poet John Cooper Clarke, are like stand-up comedians – but instead of telling jokes, they recite their funny poems.

What are the poem's themes?

A poem's themes are the ideas the poet is interested in and wants the reader to focus on. The themes might be shown through a character's words, the poet's own voice, or what happens in the poem. A poet's themes are sometimes linked to his or her judgements about how people live. For example, Lindsay MacRae's poem "My Sister Turned into Barbie" (page 47) expresses her views on contemporary values.

What is the poem's context?

The context of a poem is the time and place in which it was written. Where and when the poet lived, and what life was like at the time, can shine a light on the poem's **purpose** and theme. In the 1840s, when Edward Lear was writing his limericks, the society in which he lived was very **repressed**. There were lots of rules governing manners, which meant some people could not be themselves. For example, children were meant to be "seen and not heard". In many of Lear's limericks, one of his themes seems to be people who behave as they like. As you read them, think about whether Lear has a message, such as:

- People are often punished if they try to have fun
- Independent people should be admired
- A world without rules would be a happier place.

PACT

A good technique for analysing most types of poems is called "PACT" (it does not always work for very short comic poems). When analysing a poem, think of questions linked to each letter:

Purpose	Audience	Context	Theme
What is the purpose of the poem?	Who was the poem written for? Is there a fictional (made-up) listener in the poem?	When was the poem written? What was the poet's life and world like?	What is the main idea of the poem? What is the poem's message?

Limericks

Nonsense poetry became very popular in the 1800s. It was often written in short stanzas that people could remember easily and recite (speak aloud as a performance). The most famous form of nonsense verse is called the limerick. Limericks often begin with the phrase "There was a ...". They are frequently about a character that sounds so odd, they are unlikely to be real. But a real place name is often given for where the character comes from.

Limericks from A Book of Nonsense

by Edward Lear

There was a Young Lady of Norway,
Who casually sat on a doorway;
When the door squeezed her flat,
She exclaimed, "What of that?"
This courageous Young Lady of Norway.

There was an Old Person of Dutton,
Whose head was as small as a button,
So, to make it look big,
He purchased a wig,
And rapidly rushed about Dutton.

Edward Lear's A Book of Nonsense included over 200 limericks, each illustrated with a hilarious pen and ink drawing. This one depicts "An Old Person of Dutton".

What is a limerick?

Spotting a limerick is easy because limericks have special features. Limericks usually have five lines. In early limericks, the fifth line is often a repeat of the first line – or repeats several words from the first line. The words at the ends of the lines rhyme.

In Lear's limericks, lines 1, 2, and 5 rhyme (Dutton, button, Dutton), and lines 3 and 4 rhyme (big, wig). The rhythm or beat of a poem depends on which words or parts of words (**syllables**) are **stressed** or emphasized when you speak it aloud. The limerick often uses a pattern of three stressed syllables in lines 1, 2, and 5, and two stressed syllables in lines 3 and 4. The stressed syllables are marked:

> There <u>was</u> an Old <u>Per</u>son of <u>Dut</u>ton,
> Whose <u>head</u> was as <u>small</u> as a <u>but</u>ton,
> So, to <u>make</u> it look <u>big</u>,
> He <u>pur</u>chased a <u>wig</u>,
> And <u>ra</u>pidly <u>rushed</u> about <u>Dut</u>ton.

Limerick beginnings

It is thought that the limerick was invented in the village of Croom near the town of Limerick (pictured here) in Ireland, in the 1700s. A group of fun-loving poets made up words to an old Irish tune to make each other laugh. The way the words and parts of words were emphasized to follow the beat of the music gave the verse form its swinging, song-like sound. The beat and nonsensical content became very popular, especially after Edward Lear's *A Book of Nonsense* was published in 1845.

IDENTIFYING THE RHYTHM

To find the rhythm in a poem, read the poem aloud. Clap or tap each time you find you say a word, or part of a word, more loudly. Then underline these, as they are the stressed syllables.

Lear's life and times

It is useful to look at the context (time and setting) in which Lear's limericks were written. Lear lived in England during the reign of Queen Victoria (1837–1901). During this period, there were detailed rules about how to behave. For example, a wealthy woman would be thought **vulgar** if she pulled out a chair to sit on. She had to wait for a man to do it.

This context helps us understand Lear's choice of subject – **quirky** characters. His limerick characters are based on how people behaved in this society, and how absurd or funny the people were that followed all the rules. He also wrote about likeable **eccentrics** who refused to **conform**. The strange Young Lady of Norway was "courageous" and did not sit where she should do. She did not even care that she was flattened ("What of that?")! Lear himself was shy and sometimes felt he had to hide away because he did not want people to know he suffered from **seizures**. Perhaps he wished that he was more courageous, too.

In the 1800s, cartoonists and writers often made fun of society. This 1827 cartoon, called "Monstrosities", makes fun of the ridiculous fashions of the day. The women's hats are decorated with huge bows, feathers, and flowers, while their waists are pinched right in by tight corsets.

EDWARD LEAR

1812–1888

Born: Holloway, Middlesex, England

Edward Lear was an English artist, traveller, and writer who became well known for his limericks and nonsense verse. Perhaps his most famous nonsense poem is "The Owl and the Pussycat" (1867).

Did you know?
Although Lear's work shows that he had a great sense of humour, he suffered from depression and loneliness throughout his life.

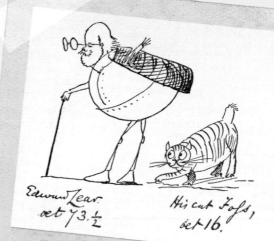

Edwarw Lear. æt 73½

His cat Foss, æt 16.

Lear often made fun of himself in illustrations like this. In a poem called "How Pleasant to Know Mr. Lear", he describes himself as having a "remarkably big" nose and a face that is "more or less hideous".

Think about this

Is Lear making fun of his characters?

In the limericks on page 8, do you think Lear is making fun of his characters or praising them? Consider his life and the society he lived in. The Old Person rushed off to buy a wig. Why do you think he did this? Was it because he was vain or because society had a rule about how people should look? Perhaps Lear's feelings about his own appearance would make him feel sorry for a person with an unusually small head. The Young Lady sat "casually … on a doorway". Did Lear see her as a silly fool or a risk-taker?

Burgess's nonsense

Later limerick writers, such as Frank Gelett Burgess, did not always follow the same limerick form as Edward Lear. Some used different openings from "There was ...". Some kept the same opening but did not repeat much of the first line in the last line. These slightly different forms allowed for more comedy.

What makes Burgess's limerick "I'd Rather Have Fingers than Toes" (see opposite) "nonsense verse"? The poet's thoughts are whimsical (playful) and silly. Few people spend time thinking which they prefer – their toes or fingers! Nonsense verse is usually funny. The energetic rhythm of this limerick emphasizes the humour and keeps phrases like "Awfully Sad" light. If Burgess used a slower rhythm and a phrase like "horrified", the mood would be gloomy. Similarly, the verse would be less funny (and more thoughtful) if each line did not end with a rhyming word. As with Lear's limericks, Burgess's were written for children, so perhaps we should not look for any serious ideas in the nonsense. Or perhaps they contain important ideas or themes that the writer did not even plan.

FRANK GELETT BURGESS

1866–1951
Born: Boston, Massachusetts, USA

Frank Gelett Burgess was an American artist, art critic, humourist, and poet whose nonsense poetry became popular in the 1890s.

Did you know? Burgess invented the word "blurb" (which means the text on the back of a book that tells you about the contents).

In 1924, Burgess started a popular comic strip, called Goops. It featured strange, bald-headed creatures called Goops.

Limerick

by Frank Gelett Burgess

I'd rather have Fingers than Toes
I'd rather have Ears than a Nose
  As for my Hair
  I'm Glad it's All There;
I'll be Awfully Sad when it Goes!

Limerick

by Ogden Nash

A jolly young fellow from Yuma
Told an elephant joke to a puma;
Now his skeleton lies
Beneath hot western skies –
The puma had no sense of huma.

OGDEN NASH

1902–1971
Born: Rye, New York, USA

Ogden Nash was an American poet who became well known for his humorous poems in which he played with words to create **tongue-twisters** and brief, memorable statements called **epigrams**.

Did you know? It's said that in reply to critics of his poems, Nash said, "I'm a worsifier, not a versifier." Perhaps by "worsifier" he meant that he deliberately distorted grammar, rhyme, and **metre**, and misspelt and made up words. He chose to break the rules.

To celebrate 100 years since his birth, in 2002 the US Postal Service released a stamp featuring Ogden Nash.

Breaking the rules

Ogden Nash's light-hearted limerick (above) shows a delight in the sound and feel of words. His made-up spelling for humour ("huma") seems to make fun of the humourless puma, like in a playground chant (puma/huma). We don't know what the elephant joke was, but since the man is described as "jolly" we can have no sympathy for the puma who kills him!

"Jabberwocky"

"Jabberwocky" is often described as the most famous of nonsense poems. While Lear's limericks are both funny and nonsensical, "Jabberwocky" is exciting and – although it contains many made-up words – we can just about make sense of it. Read through it, and you will find that, put together, the unfamiliar words create a mysterious mood and haunting images.

"Jabberwocky" first appeared in Lewis Carroll's novel for children *Through the Looking-Glass, and What Alice Found There*. Published in 1871, the novel was a sequel to *Alice's Adventures in Wonderland*, also by Lewis Carroll. The child, Alice, discovers the poem in the back-to-front world in which her mysterious adventures are set.

A QUICK READ-THROUGH

If a poem is difficult to understand, it is useful to first read through it once or twice without pausing. You will pick up the mood of the poem, and pictures may begin to form in your mind. This gives a good base from which to investigate the poem in detail.

Although we can never be sure what a Jabberwock looks like, the artist and cartoonist John Tenniel drew what came into his mind. This illustration is one of many in Carroll's book *Through the Looking-Glass*.

"Jabberwocky"

by Lewis Carroll

'Twas brillig, and the slithy toves
    Did gyre and gimble in the wabe;
All mimsy were the borogoves,
    And the mome raths outgrabe.

"Beware the Jabberwock, my son!
    The jaws that bite, the claws that catch!
Beware the Jubjub bird, and shun
    The frumious Bandersnatch!"

He took his vorpal sword in hand;
    Long time the manxome foe he sought—
So rested he by the Tumtum tree
    And stood awhile in thought.

And, as in uffish thought he stood,
    The Jabberwock, with eyes of flame,
Came whiffling through the tulgey wood,
    And burbled as it came!

One, two! One, two! And through and through
    The vorpal blade went snicker-snack!
He left it dead, and with its head
    He went galumphing back.

"And hast thou slain the Jabberwock?
    Come to my arms, my beamish boy!
O frabjous day! Callooh! Callay!"
    He chortled in his joy.

'Twas brillig, and the slithy toves
    Did gyre and gimble in the wabe:
All mimsy were the borogoves,
    And the mome raths outgrabe.

What was a Jabberwock? Perhaps Lewis Carroll's creature, and the illustrator Tenniel's picture, were inspired by the models of dinosaurs that went on display in a hugely popular exhibition in Crystal Palace, London, in 1854. They were the world's first dinosaur sculptures.

Nonce words

Many of the words in "Jabberwocky" are **nonce words**. These are words that have no clear meaning and are not in any dictionary when the writer first uses them. Sometimes, nonce words become popular and, as they are used, their meaning becomes defined. Two nonce words in "Jabberwocky" have become established words in the English language and now appear in dictionaries. These words are "chortle" (chuckle gleefully) and "galumph" (gallop triumphantly). Carroll's "vorpal swords" often appear in fantasy games, where they are magic blades.

Finding meaning

From the first word of "Jabberwocky", we know we are going to be told a tale. The old-fashioned but familiar word "'Twas" (meaning "It was") is often found at the beginning of traditional tales. But then we are faced with lots of nonsense words. To have a guess at the meaning of a nonce, it's useful to look at 1) its make-up, spelling, and sound; 2) neighbouring words; and 3) its position in a whole sentence.

1 Some nonce words have a similar spelling or sound to a real word, which gives us a clue to their meaning: "brill" in "brillig" is like "brilliant" or "bright"; "slithy" sounds like "lithe" (graceful or slim) and "slimy", so perhaps it is a combination of both.
2 If "slithy" means lithe and slimy then it must be an adjective – and in "slithy toves" it is describing what the "toves" are like. This is a clue to the meaning of "toves". "Toves" sounds like the word "toads", and an amphibian might well be described as slimy. But it's a lithe amphibian, so perhaps a "slithy tove" is a kind of slimy newt.

3 Sentences always have a noun and a verb or verbs. We have found the noun (toves) and so "gyre and gimble" must be the verbs describing what the toves are doing. "Gyre" means revolve, and "gimble" sounds like gambol (to skip or dance playfully). So perhaps the newts are spiralling and leaping. Sentences often contain extra information, and "in the" suggests that "in the wabe" sets the scene (perhaps "wabe" is woods or another sort of habitat). It is because "Jabberwocky" uses grammar correctly (for example, with nouns and adjectives in logical places) that we get a sense of the meaning of the poem.

MAKE NOTES

To try to work out meanings, it is useful to annotate a poem with notes:

This sets the scene for the story: It was bright/brilliant (perhaps sunny or moonlit)

An adjective that describes the toves: lithe and slimy

The noun: something like a newt

'Twas brillig, and the slithy toves
Did gyre and gimble in the wabe;

The verbs: spiral and gambol or leap

The setting: woods

The joy of words

When Alice goes to Humpty for advice on the meaning of "Jabberwocky", Humpty comes up with some different ideas from those we worked out on the previous pages. For example, he says: "'BRILLIG' means four o'clock in the afternoon—the time when you begin BROILING things for dinner." Humpty's meanings for other nonce words are also imaginative. He thinks "borogove" may be "a thin shabby-looking bird with its feathers sticking out all round—something like a live mop". He suggests "outgrabing" is "something between bellowing and whistling, with a kind of sneeze in the middle".

Lewis Carroll is having fun with words, teasing his readers with definitions to show that the words in "Jabberwocky" could really mean anything. Have a go at writing your own definitions, or make up some new words for your own "Jabberwocky"-style poem.

In *Through the Looking-Glass*, the character of Alice goes to Humpty for advice on the meaning of the poem "Jabberwocky".

Think about this
Why is "Jabberwocky" so popular?

Why do you think that "Jabberwocky" is so popular when it is impossible to be sure what most of it means? How many reasons can you think of?

Writer's tricks

Lewis Carroll uses lots of tricks in "Jabberwocky" to make the words appealing and draw the reader in:

- He squashes two words together (called a portmanteau). Example: slimy and lithe are put together to create a word that means both ("slithy").
- He uses words that sound like the thing named (onomatopoeia). Example: "snicker-snack" sounds like swords striking each other.
- He repeats a similar vowel sound (assonance). Example: the gentle "o-e" sounds in "toves", "borogoves", and "mome" have a mysterious echo-like effect.
- He repeats consonants (**alliteration**). Example: In "Callooh! Callay!" the repetition of "c" sounds crisp, like a shout.

CHARLES LUTWIDGE DODGSON;
PEN NAME LEWIS CARROLL

1832–1898
Born: Daresbury, Cheshire, England

Charles Dodgson was an English logician, mathematician, photographer, and novelist. He published his famous *Alice's Adventures in Wonderland* (1865) and *Through the Looking-Glass, and What Alice Found There* (1871) under the pen name Lewis Carroll.

Did you know? Dodgson had a stammer and was always shy in adult company.

Charles Dodgson invented many board games, including a word game that was similar to today's Scrabble.

Haiku

Haiku is a 400-year-old form of poetry, which started in Japan. Traditionally it creates intense feelings about nature. But the concept can also be parodied to create a very funny poem.

Parody is a form of humour. Television comics who mimic well-known people are using parody to entertain their audience. Parody is a way of drawing attention to an element of a person, idea, or concept to make people laugh. Certain features or words might be imitated while others are made fun of. For example, the verse on page 5 ("Twinkle, Twinkle, Little Bat") is a parody of "Twinkle, Twinkle, Little Star".

The target for a laugh

To fully enjoy a parody of a **haiku**, it is helpful to know what readers expect from this form of poetry. Common features are:

- A short form of three lines (5 syllables in lines 1 and 3; 7 syllables in line 2)
- Two **contrasting** (different) images
- A word that separates the two images
- Imagery that captures a moment in nature.

Haiku
by Matsuo Bashō

Old pond
leap – splash
a frog.

A frog disturbs the calm of a peaceful old pond.

MATSUO BASHŌ

1644–1694

Born: Ueno, Iga Province, Japan

Matsuo Bashō was a Japanese poet whose haiku were greatly admired and who made the haiku a popular form of poetry.

Did you know? Matsuo Bashō gave up his position as a samurai (Japanese warrior) to become a full-time poet.

In this 19th-century Japanese woodcut, the artist imagines Matsuo Bashō stopping to have tea with two men by the roadside.

The 17th-century haiku shown opposite is by the Japanese poet Matsuo Bashō. This is a translation (from Japanese to English) so it no longer has the traditional number of syllables that it has in its Japanese form. The contrasting images are: "Old pond" (the fact that the pond is old suggests that it is still, quiet, and overgrown, and perhaps hidden away from life and activity); and "splash" (a splash is a very different image from an undisturbed old pond, and represents sudden activity and life). The word "leap" separates the two images – the frog leaping causes the change to the scene.

Humorous haiku

Not all of Bashō's haiku was serious. In the haiku below, we can imagine a poet who is happy to laugh at himself and who would enjoy the slapstick humour of slipping and sliding in the snow and ice:

Now then, let's go out
to enjoy the snow ... until
I slip and fall!

Haiku

by Janie Milton

Misty tree-tops, peace
Screech! From branch to branch, swinging
 – a meringue-utan!

Comparing haiku

The poem above is a contemporary parody of Bashō's frog haiku. By comparing a haiku with its parody we can test how successful the parody is. There should be similarities, but there should also be differences that make the reader laugh. Here is a comparison chart:

The meringue-utan is a fictional funny creature invented by Janie Milton.

Feature	Bashō's haiku	Contemporary haiku
Does it have a traditional 3-line 5, 7, 5 syllable form?	Original Japanese text had the traditional form	Yes
Opening 1st image	Yes: old pond	Yes: misty, peaceful tree-tops
Contrasting 2nd image	Yes: splashing frog	Yes: screeching, vaulting meringue-utan
Word that splits the images	Yes: splash	Yes: screech
Concluding line	A frog	A meringue-utan!

The two haiku are similar in lots of ways – so what makes the contemporary haiku funny? The meringue-utan is a pun on orangutan. This is emphasized by its position in the last line – like the last line of a joke. A meringue-utan is a made-up creature like the Jabberwock and Jubjub bird in "Jabberwocky". But unlike the Jubjub and the Jabberwock, we can more or less imagine what a meringue-utan looks like – so a meringue-utan is funny on two levels: it is a play on words and it paints a funny image in the reader's mind.

Think about this

How can imagery involve all the senses?

Building a mental picture with words is called imagery. However, the most effective imagery involves more than just a visual image – it draws in some of the other senses, too (hearing, touch, taste, smell). The imagery found in Bashō's haiku below involves several senses in just a few words:

> Sleep on horseback,
> The far moon in a continuing dream,
> Steam of roasting tea.

The reader's imagination is inspired to "feel" the horse, the sensation of being asleep and dreaming, and the warmth and the smell of the tea.

COUNTING SYLLABLES

To count the syllables in a word, say the word out loud and split it into its separate sounds. For example: screech/ing or o/rang/u/tan. If you are still unsure of the number of syllables in a word, you can check in a dictionary. Many dictionaries show words split into syllables.

"Serious Luv"

Humour often comes from the voice of the speaker in a poem. A character's voice allows us to hear their thoughts and see the world through their eyes. In "Serious Luv" by Benjamin Zephaniah, the poet writes as if he were still at school.

Monologue

"Serious Luv" is a humorous **monologue** – we know it's a monologue because it's written in the first person (using words like "me" and "I"). A monologue involves an audience (the reader or listener). It often takes the form of the speaker "saying" their thoughts aloud and expressing their opinions as if in conversation with the reader or listener.

In "Serious Luv", instead of being told by the poet what he was like as a boy, we have to decide for ourselves by reading what the "boy" himself says and how he says it. The events, ideas, experiences, and opinions in the poem tell us a lot about Benjamin Zephaniah as a schoolboy. But the style of the poem tells us even more. This is why it is important to look at the choice of **vocabulary**, spelling, and use of rhyme and rhythm. They are all clues to his character and add to the humour.

All over the world, teenagers sometimes use graffiti to express their "luv". *Te amo* means "I love you".

24

"Serious Luv"

by Benjamin Zephaniah

Monday Morning
I really luv de girl dat's sitting next to me
I think she thinks like me an she's so cool,
I think dat we could live forever happily
I want to marry her when I leave school.

She's de only one in school allowed to call me Ben
When she does Maths I luv de way she chews her Pen,
When we are doing Art she's so artistic
In Biology she makes me heart beat so quick.

When we do Geography I go to paradise
She's helped me draw a map of Borneo twice!
Today she's going to help me take me books home
So I am going to propose to her when we're alone.

The next day
I used to luv de girl dat's sitting next to me
But yesterday it all came to an end,
She said that I should take love more seriously
An now I think I really luv her friend.

POINT, EVIDENCE, EXPLAIN (P.E.E.)

Do you think that the girl liked Ben? To answer questions
like this, use the P.E.E. method:

1 State your point.
2 Back it up with evidence (such as a quoted word or
   phrase from the poem).
3 Explain what the evidence tells us in more detail. For
   example, in your answer to the question you could make
   the point that we don't know for sure what the girl feels.
   Then you could **quote** the evidence: "Today she's going
   to help me take me books home". Then you could explain
   that this proves nothing – she could just be being kind.

Serious love?

The poem is about love. On a first read-through, which is the funniest part? Is it where we discover how quickly Ben falls out of love and then in love with a different girl? Looking closer, we find that we slowly learn more about his relationship with the first girl. He gives lots of reasons for why he loves her, such as "I think she thinks like me". But he only "thinks" – he doesn't know for certain. Perhaps he doesn't even know the girl very well.

There is a lack of any evidence that Ben is kind to the girl. All he says is that he lets her call him Ben, while she carries his books home! She thinks he doesn't take love seriously – and then he proves it in the final line of the poem by saying he loves someone else the very next day. The humour lies in his not realizing the wisdom of her words. He does not question his feelings at all.

Spellings

The spellings of that ("dat"), the ("de"), and my ("me") give a clue as to the boy's **accent**, which is Jamaican. These words are spelt **phonetically** – in the way a Jamaican would speak them. A sense of the boy's accent helps us to hear his voice and brings him to life.

There is **irony** in the poem's title. Irony is the use of words to suggest a meaning that is the opposite of the one expressed. The irony in this poem lies in the difference between what Ben meant by the title and what he actually wrote. "Love" is usually only spelt "luv" in the context of passing school crushes – not in the context of "serious" lasting love. Ben thinks the poem is about the "serious" love he feels, but in writing "luv" and not "love" he is revealing the opposite.

BENJAMIN ZEPHANIAH

1958–

Born: Birmingham, West Midlands, England

Although Benjamin Zephaniah himself has a regional English accent, when performing he speaks with a Jamaican accent.

Benjamin Zephaniah is a British Jamaican **Rastafarian**. He is a poet, writer, **lyricist**, musician, and dub poet (a dub poet performs poetry in a special West Indian style to a background of reggae music rhythms).

Did you know? Zephaniah was severely dyslexic and left school at 13 unable to read or write. By the age of 15, he was already well known in the city of Birmingham as a dub poetry performer.

Rhyme

The form of "Serious Luv" matches the schoolboy voice. The boy is so desperate to make the poem rhyme that he has fallen into the trap of choosing words that sound silly:

- In stanza 1, the phrase "forever happily" sounds odd because we would always say "happily forever".
- In stanza 2, the line "When we are doing Art she's so artistic" is funny because the word "artistic" is such an unimaginative choice. It rhymes, but the repetition of a word ("art", "art"-istic) makes it fall flat.
- In stanza 3, "twice" is funny – it seems unlikely he had to draw Borneo twice, so perhaps he used "twice" just because he needed a word that rhymed with "paradise".

Rhythm

Try reading the poem as you tap the rhythm with a pencil. You will hear the parts that sound good and the parts that sound awkward. To "scan" a poem is to work out if it has a regular rhythm – if it doesn't have one then you can say, "This line/stanza/poem doesn't scan." In stanza 2, for example, Zephaniah uses a strong, regular beat in the first two lines that is easy to read aloud. But the third, shorter line sounds clunky, and it is easy to stumble over the longer, three-syllable word "artistic":

> She's de only one in school allowed to call me Ben
> When she does Maths I luv de way she chews her Pen,
> When we are doing Art she's so artistic

After reading the whole poem, the reader feels that "Ben" hasn't written a brilliant love poem but that he is likeable because he has made such an effort.

FEET AND METRES

To write about the rhythm of a poem, it is useful to understand the meaning of the words "feet" and "metres". But don't worry too much about the technical details: for now it's enough just to know that feet and metres affect the sound and feeling of a poem.

- A **foot** is a set of stressed and unstressed syllables. There are different types of feet: for example, da-DUM (called an iam), DUM-da (called a trochee), da-da-DUM (called an anapest).
- Metre refers to the type of foot and the number of these in each line. For example, iambic tetrameter is 4 sets of da-DUM. Anapestic trimeter is 3 sets of da-da-DUM. Lear's limericks are in anapestic trimeter.

Think about this
What would make the love seem real?

How would you change "Serious Luv" to make it seem that Ben's feelings were real love and not a passing crush? Think about the vocabulary and how you might change the ending.

What is serious luv? "Serious Luv" takes a humorous look at Ben's and a girl's views.

"Sick"

In the 1974 poem "Sick" by Shel Silverstein, a little girl wants to stay in bed and not go to school. From time to time, most children – and many adults – feel this way about getting out of bed in the morning. The first question to ask yourself when you read the poem is: Is it funny?

Is it funny?

Your first reaction as to whether you find a poem funny or not is very important. Humour often relies on surprise, so when you read a poem again some of the humour might disappear. After a first or second reading, note down the lines that you found funny. Or underline phrases or words that made you smile, or those that did not seem to work. These notes will help you to judge the poem fairly as you investigate it further.

Different things make different people laugh, so there is no correct answer to how funny a poem is. Everyone's opinion is of value as long as his or her reasons are backed up with evidence from the poem. So always remember to collect quotations to back up your views about a poem.

Think about this
What if it doesn't make you laugh?

If a humorous poem does not make you laugh, it does not necessarily mean it's a bad poem. While you might not find a poem funny, perhaps someone else would, such as a younger reader or an adult. If the poem was written a long time ago, its original audience might have found it funny. So when judging the success of a poem, think about whether it is well written or well structured, and consider the audience it was written for.

"Sick"

by Shel Silverstein

"I cannot go to school today,"
Said little Peggy Ann McKay.
"I have the measles and the mumps,
A gash, a rash and purple bumps.
My mouth is wet, my throat is dry,
I'm going blind in my right eye.
My tonsils are as big as rocks,
I've counted sixteen chicken pox
And there's one more – that's seventeen,
And don't you think my face looks green?
My leg is cut – my eyes are blue –
It might be instamatic flu.
I cough and sneeze and gasp and choke,
I'm sure that my left leg is broke –
My hip hurts when I move my chin,
My belly button's caving in,
My back is wrenched, my ankle's sprained,
My 'pendix pains each time it rains.
My nose is cold, my toes are numb.
I have a sliver in my thumb.
My neck is stiff, my voice is weak,
I hardly whisper when I speak.
My tongue is filling up my mouth,
I think my hair is falling out.
My elbow's bent, my spine ain't straight,
My temperature is one-o-eight.
My brain is shrunk, I cannot hear,
There is a hole inside my ear.
I have a hangnail, and my heart is – what?
What's that? What's that you say?
You say today is...Saturday?
G'bye, I'm going out to play!"

Shel Silverstein drew pictures to illustrate his poems. This illustration first appeared alongside "Sick" in his 1974 book *Where the Sidewalk Ends*.

Who is the audience?

A poet usually has the age of their readers in mind. Shel Silverstein is well known as a poet who wrote for children. Lots of evidence suggests that "Sick" is a children's poem:

- Subject: many children would be familiar with the subject of wanting to stay in bed rather than go to school.
- Structure: the **structure** is simple (an introduction followed by a long quoted monologue, with concluding lines that bring the poem to an amusing end).
- Vocabulary: the words are those that many children might use so they are easy to understand.
- Humour: funny poetry is popular with children (the long list of exaggerated illnesses and the ending are funny).

Another group of people might find the poem funny, too: adults, especially parents, carers, or teachers. These people might be familiar with the way children try to persuade them to let them do something – or not do something, such as their homework. Also, adults might remember using the same tactics when they were young. Readers often enjoy poems because there is something in them that they recognize or are familiar with – an experience they have had themselves.

What is the purpose?

The purpose of the poem is to make us smile about a subject we, as children or adults, might be familiar with. But what is Peggy Ann McKay's purpose? Her purpose is to persuade the listener to let her stay at home, and not go to school. By looking in detail at Peggy's words, we find that her over-the-top attempt to persuade is the main source of humour.

The poem becomes a **list poem** of all Peggy's reasons why she can't go to school. The humour comes from the length of the list (it would be impossible for her to have all these illnesses). Lots of the reasons are absurd (she would be shouting out in pain if she had a broken leg!). She uses exaggeration (**hyperbole**) for **dramatic effect**, in the hope she can persuade the listener how ill she is. But the exaggerations have the reverse effect – instead of feeling increasingly worried about her, we find her more comical. Listing one very severe illness next to a tiny problem also adds to the comedy: "There is a hole inside my ear. / I have a hangnail".

Peggy's childish use of language is also comic. "Instamatic flu" is a **malapropism** (an incorrect word in place of a similar-sounding word). By "instamatic" perhaps she meant "infectious", or she might be joining the words "instant" and "automatic" to mean that her illness has suddenly come about.

SHEL SILVERSTEIN

1930–1999
Born: Chicago, Illinois, USA

Shel (Sheldon) Silverstein was an American poet, singer-songwriter, cartoonist, and screenwriter who became famous for his books for children.

Did you know? Shel Silverstein avoided happy endings in his children's stories because he was worried that children who read happy endings might wonder why they weren't happy themselves.

When interviewed about writing for children, Shel Silverstein said, "I do eliminate certain things when I'm writing for children if I think only an adult will get the idea."

Voice and listener

Most of the poem "Sick" is quoted speech from the character Peggy Ann McKay. Who is she talking to? It is only at the end that we become aware of a listener. Peggy asks questions as if someone has just spoken to her: "What's that? What's that you say? You say today is...Saturday?" We can imagine a parent or carer listening to her non-stop list of reasons, or trying to interrupt to explain that it's Saturday so there is no school anyway!

The fact that it is a Saturday is a surprise to both the reader and Peggy. But the concluding joke is the speed with which Peggy recovers from all her illnesses, and rushes off to play. Like the imagined listener, the reader is left feeling both amazed and amused at Peggy's complete recovery.

Like Peggy, these little girls have "measles", a "rash", and "purple bumps".

Rhyme and rhythm of speech

How effective are the rhyme and rhythm? Do they help us to imagine Peggy's voice? Her speech is in rhyming couplets (pairs of lines that rhyme and are of the same length):

> *My brain is shrunk, I cannot hear,*
> *There is a hole inside my ear.*

The rhyming only breaks off when Peggy is interrupted and she addresses the listener: "I have a hangnail, and my heart is – what?" The word "what" does not rhyme with the line above or below, so it is a clever way of showing how Peggy has been interrupted.

The rhythm also reflects Peggy's speech. As in "Serious Luv", the poet uses the iamb foot four times per line (iambic tetrameter):

> *I have the measles and the mumps,*
> *A gash, a rash and purple humps.*

The iamb foot is simple and light, making it useful for a child's voice in a humorous poem. Iambic tetrameter is often used in **ballads** and has a sing-song sound suitable for "little" Peggy. It also makes you read the poem quite quickly – which makes it seem as if Peggy is rushing to get in as many reasons as possible not to go to school before the listener interrupts.

Think about this
Which is your favourite?

Which poem did you enjoy most – "Sick" or "Serious Luv"? See how many reasons you can find to explain your opinion. For example: Which subject was most familiar to you? Which character could you most easily imagine as real? Which poem had the most effective vocabulary? Don't forget that each of your reasons must be backed up with evidence.

"Ice Cream War"

S ome poems are subtle in both their humour and their swordplay. "Ice Cream War" by the Mexican-American poet Gary Soto is one of those poems. When you read it through, look out for the hidden basketball puns. Like in "Serious Luv" on page 25, the voice in the poem is that of a youngster.

"Ice Cream War"

by Gary Soto

I thought, OK, one scoop,
And then my friend said, "Two scoops, sir."

I changed my mind.
I said, "No, two scoops, chocolate and pistachio."

My friend shooed away a fly,
Wiggled the front of his T-shirt
Damp from one-on-one basketball.
He said, "Correction—three scoops!"

I said, "Four, with alternate strawberry and melon flavors!"
Then he said, "Five, any flavor!"

The line behind us got long,
I nudged my friend, "Hey, we better hurry."
We ended up tied: four scoops on a tiny cone,
A balancing act.
When I reached into my pocket
I only had enough for three scoops.
Quadruple trouble! I had already licked
The top scoop, coffee-mocha flavor.
The boy behind the counter,
The one in an apron stained like a rainbow,
The one I had been calling "Sir,"
Tapped his shoe,
Waiting.

I unscrewed the top scoop,
Said, "Here, sir. I forgot—
Mom says I'm too young for coffee."

Compare voices

We know that the speaker in "Ice Cream War" is young because he says his mother thinks he is "too young" for coffee (health professionals believe that the caffeine in coffee is bad for children). There is no proof that the speaker is a boy and not a girl. But the speaker's friend is male ("He said") and as they are playing basketball together it seems likely that it is a boy (although, of course, girls play and like basketball, too).

"Serious Luv" and "Ice Cream War" have similar voices, but how else are the narrators the same or different? Think about: their interests, their characteristics, what issues they face, and their vocabulary. It may help to draw a table with rows for these issues and columns for the two poems. Back up your ideas with evidence.

WORD BANK

How many of the terms below (or parts of them) can you find in "Ice Cream War"? The phrases are often used in basketball or other sports:

Fly ball – a batted ball that is hit into the air in basketball
Licked – got the better of, or beaten
Quadruple double – an amazing feat for a basketball player to achieve (only four players have done so in the National Basketball Association). In a single game, a player has to achieve 10 or more in four of these categories: points, assists, rebounds, steals, or blocked shots.
Scoop shot – a shot of the ball made with an underhand scooping motion
Shoot – the aim of basketball is to shoot (push) a ball through a basket
Tap – strike the ball in the direction of a team member or towards the basket
Tie – finish a game with both teams having the same score, and no clear winner; in basketball, extra time might be played until one team gets a higher score.

Free verse

Unlike "Serious Luv", Soto's poem is written in **free verse** – a form of poetry that does not have regular rhyming words or a regular metre. The free verse means that there are no humorously jarring rhythms or rhyming words like there are in "Serious Luv". "Ice Cream War" is made up of a dialogue. This makes the whole poem less formal and it reads almost like prose. But it is a poem and not prose, so the lengths of the lines and where they break are important.

The line breaks and stanza breaks create short or long pauses. For example, the pause created by starting a new stanza after line 2 creates the thinking time in which the speaker changes his mind. There are also pauses (using a comma and short lines) to create the effect of waiting in the **penultimate** stanza:

> *The one I had been calling "Sir,"*
> *Tapped his shoe,*
> *Waiting.*

Line length helps give the sense of real dialogue, with a new line starting after each set of spoken words. Line length is also used for dramatic effect. In the example below, the short line and the pause after the full stop, help the reader imagine the wobbling ice cream:

> *A balancing act.*

Metaphor

A **metaphor** compares two unalike things without using words such as "like" or "as". An example is in calling someone an "early bird" because they get up early. They are not a bird at all, but they get up early, like a bird. "Ice Cream War" is an extended metaphor – Soto compares basketball with buying ice cream. He keeps the link going throughout the poem by using basketball words.

The climax of the poem ("Quadruple trouble!") is a pun on the basketball term "quadruple double". Other words that link with basketball are "scoops", "shooed away a fly", and "tied". The title "Ice Cream War" suggests that the boys are competing in their ice cream eating, just as they have been in their sport. In the end, the speaker has to return the top scoop, but he has not really lost the ice cream "war" because he has "already licked" it!

GARY SOTO

1952–

Born: Fresno, California, USA

Gary Soto is a poet, essayist, and novelist, and one of the most important Mexican-American writers of his generation.

Did you know? Soto's grandparents were born in Mexico but moved to live and work in the USA. Soto's father died when he was five years old and he was brought up by his mother and older brother.

While he was growing up, Soto's family struggled for money. He had to neglect his schoolwork in order to work in the fields for extra cash.

"Third and Last"

Do you have brothers and sisters? The poet Cristin O'Keefe Aptowicz has an older brother and sister. The poem "Third and Last" describes her experiences as the youngest child in the family. The poem is about the poet's life – it is autobiographical. The poet's purpose is to paint a picture of her childhood, and draw conclusions from it.

Family life

Poets often write about their childhood – looking back at their past, often using old photographs as a starting point. In "Third and Last", O'Keefe Aptowicz draws a series of dramatic word pictures of specific childhood events (for example, her brother "lobbing" shoes into her crib). Also, she refers to images of herself in the past (in "home videos" and "old photo albums") and her brother "remembering a time" before she was born.

Cristin O'Keefe Aptowicz was three years old when this photograph was taken of her with her older brother and sister. She is in her thirties now and has written five published poetry books about her life.

"Third and Last"

by Cristin O'Keefe Aptowicz

When I was born, the disruption caused
my brother to protest, lobbing endless arcs
of shoes into my crib. Squinting, he says

he can still remember a time before me.
Mom often jokes that after having a boy
and a girl, the next logical step would've

been to get a golden retriever. But instead
I arrived: a shrill pudge forever destined
to be the yellow crayon mark in my mother's

Halloween costume idea. Home videos
show I was a child with a persistent state
of moping, my wide eyes always teary

and on the lookout for gross injustice.
These injustices, or at least those that
were recorded on film, include:

having my birthday candles cruelly
blown out by my older sister repeatedly
on my third birthday; being viciously

knocked over in an inexplicable hula
contest on our front lawn; and a walk
of shame after I peed in my ironically

yellow snowsuit during the annual
Christmas tree hunt. Today, when
friends look through old photo albums,

They have trouble finding me. It's easy,
I say, just look for the one purposefully
having no fun, the one with the bad

self-given haircut, the one crying over
her ugly jack-o-lantern, the one whose
pout seems suspiciously practiced,

the one that looks like the answer
to the question: *Come on, how bad
could having one more kid be?*

What's in a title?

If a poem has a title, it often holds a clue as to the poem's main theme. After reading a poem, it is worth looking at the poem's title again. What is the link between the title and the content of the poem? Does the title sum up the poem? Or is the title only a teaser, added just to make you want to read the poem?

After reading the poem, the title "Third and Last" takes on extra meaning. As the "third" child to be born, the poet describes how she is teased and upset – she's the "last" in line of importance. The title is a play on the often used phrase "first and last". There is an element of dark humour in this (dark humour is a way of looking at sad or serious subjects in a light-hearted way). Although amusing, the poem considers the serious theme of family relationships and siblings (brothers and sisters). The youngest in the family can sometimes get a raw deal!

Among the poet's list of childhood woes is being "knocked over in an inexplicable hula contest".

Powerful words and pathos

To create strong images in poetry, you need powerful words. Cristin O'Keefe Aptowicz uses powerful words that heighten the images that are created in the reader's mind. For example, she chooses "lobbing" instead of a more common verb like "throwing" in the phrase "lobbing endless arcs of shoes". "Lobbing" is better, as it suggests a repeated, casual chucking. She includes two adjectives in the phrase "bad / self-given haircut". "Bad haircut" alone does not tell us as much. A "self-given" haircut sounds messier.

One purpose of poetry is to make the reader feel something. What do you feel while reading "Third and Last"? There are many phrases and images that make us feel sorry for the poet as a child. This is called **pathos**. Pathos is anything in writing that makes the reader feel sadness, pity, or sympathy. Phrases like "my wide eyes always teary" show how the poet cannot stand up for herself and that she is nearly always sad. To read that she has a "self-given" haircut suggests that she felt no one bothered to cut it for her – or that she just did it for attention.

Think about this
What do you think?

One purpose of a poem is to express an idea or ideas, and to make the reader think. What thoughts do you have after re-reading "Third and Last"? The main theme of the poem is about being the youngest child in a family. Do you think it is unfair that she was treated badly? For example, when her sister "cruelly" blew out her candles? Should the mother have joked about expecting to get a dog ("golden retriever"), and that the poet came as a surprise baby? The poem can lead to a thoughtful debate about the role and responsibilities of older siblings and mothers.

Where's the humour?

In the poem "Sick" on page 31, we saw how exaggeration (hyperbole) can be very funny. In this poem, humorous hyperbole is used to describe the poet's childhood experiences. In places, there is evidence that the poet is laughing at herself, for example when she uses overblown language such as "cruelly" and "injustice". There is slapstick comedy, too, in these lines:

> *... being viciously*
>
> *knocked over in an inexplicable hula*
> *contest on our front lawn;*

The words "viciously" and "inexplicable" sound extreme compared to the safe setting of a "front lawn". From these words, we start to suspect that she is exaggerating. When she describes her pout as "suspiciously practiced", she is admitting that as a child she sometimes pretended to look miserable. Perhaps she was just trying to get sympathy or attention, and was not unhappy at all?

Breaking sentences

In "Third and Last", sentences cross over from one stanza to another. This is called **enjambment**. Enjambment allows the poet to keep the verse form and place key words at the line ends rather than put them where they would fall in prose sentences. It also means the breaks between lines are skipped over when reading: in "Third and Last" the remembered images spill from the poet's mind with speed. We see that she is feeling emotional as she recalls her childhood. More formal breaks between stanzas would make us feel she was more controlled.

Think about this

Are there other viewpoints?

Thinking about other characters' viewpoints can help reveal contrasting ideas in a poem. How would you feel if you were the brother and had a new sister who: "caused disruption" (line 1), was "shrill" (line 8), made random yellow crayon marks (line 9), was always "on the lookout for gross injustice" (line 13), and randomly "peed" (line 21)? Try role-playing with a friend — one of you as the poet, one as the brother. Talk about the events in the poem from your own viewpoint, and how you felt. Then discuss how to answer the question at the end of the poem.

CRISTIN O'KEEFE APTOWICZ

1978–
Born: Philadelphia, Pennsylvania, USA

Cristin O'Keefe Aptowicz is an American poet and writer who has become a popular performer at New York City poetry slams (competitions in which poets recite their own poems and members of the audience act as the judges).

Did you know? O'Keefe Aptowicz believes that by focusing on just an event, person, object, or emotion, a poet can give people an insight into what life for the poet was really like.

Cristin O'Keefe Aptowicz once said, "All of my poetry is autobiographical."

"My Sister Turned into Barbie"

A **symbol** in a poem is an object that stands for something else – often something important. In this humorous nonsense poem by Lindsay MacRae, the Barbie doll could be seen as a symbol. But what does the Barbie doll symbolize – what does it represent?

Becoming a Barbie

By looking closely at the text we can see that the sister starts to wear Barbie-like clothes ("skirt ... much too tight", "wearing pink a lot", "silly purple pumps"). Her body then becomes doll-like ("she had gone all stiff", a chest of "plastic lumps", hair like "flaxen rope"). The change from person to doll becomes both horrific and hilarious: her knickers are "welded on", bubbles come out of her head, and she is so stiff her limbs have to be straightened to get her into bed.

The climax comes with the "pink plastic nightmare" and the sister/doll becoming "weird under water". This is emphasized by the longer line and its position between stanzas. By dressing as a Barbie doll, she has become a Barbie doll. This is underlined in her mum's words:

> My mum said: "Take this flipping thing
> And give me back my daughter!"

The sister has become a "thing", not a daughter and not a person.

Barbie is a bestselling doll for which lots of fashion outfits can be bought. A doll called Ken was made by the same toy company and sold as Barbie's first "boyfriend".

"My Sister Turned into Barbie"

by Lindsay MacRae

My sister turned into Barbie
It happened in the night
By breakfast she had gone all stiff
And her skirt was much too tight

She started wearing pink a lot
And silly purple pumps
Where once a vest covered her chest
She now had plastic lumps

Her hair became a flaxen rope
Which hung down to her knees
Her knickers they were welded on
So she couldn't go for pees

She started hanging out with Ken
Blew bubbles from her head
We had to straighten out her limbs
To get her into bed

Life was becoming a pink plastic nightmare so…

We took her to the toy shop
When she turned weird under water
My mum said: "Take this flipping thing
And give me back my daughter!"

WRITE A PRÉCIS

To **précis** (pronounced "pray-see") means to shorten or
summarize. A good way of focusing on a poem's main idea
is to write what happens in a single sentence. "My Sister
Turned into Barbie" could be précised as: "A child's sister
turns into a plastic Barbie doll, so the mother and child take
the doll to a toy shop to swap it for the real sister." We can
then look deeper to see if the poem has a message: What is
the significance of the Barbie doll?

Cautionary tale

The Barbie doll became a popular toy in the 1960s. Children can dress her in lots of high-fashion outfits, which are often pink. Her plastic body is shaped to look good in all her clothes and her fake hair always shines. After her creation, Barbie slowly became a symbol of the lifestyle young girls wished they had. They often want her type of body, hair, clothes, and boyfriend. Many see her as "perfect" and start to dress like her. They forget that she is not real. They forget that being a real individual is more important than following the fashions of a plastic doll.

The symbolism of the Barbie doll (as an unreal thing that people try to be) is carried through the poem. The more the sister dresses and acts like Barbie, the more unreal she becomes. Perhaps the message of the poem is to be individual and not to try to become something that isn't real. The poet might also be saying that if you follow fashion too far, you will lose who you really are. The girl in the poem was lost as a daughter and a sister. "My Sister Turned into Barbie" is both a nonsense poem and a **cautionary tale**:

- It is a nonsense poem because no one would really become plastic.
- It is a cautionary tale because it is warning readers that they could lose their true self if they follow a fashion or idea too closely.

HILAIRE BELLOC'S CAUTIONARY TALES

Many cautionary tales were told in nonsense poems by Hilaire Belloc more than a hundred years ago. They were published in *Cautionary Tales for Children* (1907). Track one down and compare it with the modern-day "My Sister Turned into Barbie". Examples are: "Matilda: Who Told Lies, and was Burned to Death" and "Henry King: Who chewed bits of string, and was early cut off in Dreadful agonies".

LINDSAY MACRAE

1961–

Born: Bridlington, South Yorkshire, England

Lindsay MacRae is a Scottish poet whose poetry collections for children include *How to Make a Snail Fall in Love with You*.

Did you know? Lindsay MacRae had various jobs before she became a full-time poet. Her work included playing the saxophone and singing in pop bands.

Lindsay MacRae wrote her first poem when she was about seven years old. It was about a dog.

What have we learned?

In this book we have looked at a wide range of humorous poems. The humour varies from poem to poem – some have very funny imagery while others just have a gentle, humorous tone. Which was your favourite poem? Everyone has different tastes and a different sense of humour, so your choice of "favourite poem" might not be the same as your friend's.

Why write a poem?

We have found that humorous poems entertain, but they also have a deeper purpose. For example, "My Sister Turned into Barbie" is funny, but it also has a message (a warning to readers not to lose themselves in fashion). Other poems make us think about important subjects, too. For example, "Serious Luv" makes us think about what love really is, and how people's views of love vary.

Something absurd (like an orangutan with a meringue on its head) usually makes people laugh. Poems that cause laughter often include a surprise and something different from what you find in real life.

A poem is much more interesting if it works on more than one level. For example, if it has a message about life in general, society, or politics. Maybe it asks questions that make you think about your own life and beliefs. To find the deeper level, we need to think about the poem, re-read it, and start to look at it in detail. We need to ask questions, such as: Why did the poet spell "luv" in this way? Why did Edward Lear describe the Young Lady of Norway as "courageous"? The deeper you dig and the more you question, the more interesting the poem becomes.

How to make a reader smile

Poets use many methods to help create humour or a comic tone. Here are a few that we found:

- Characters that are funny
- Hyperbole
- Irony
- Jokes
- Lively rhythms
- Malapropisms
- Metaphor
- Nonce words
- Parody
- Slapstick imagery
- Speaker's voice
- Spellings
- Wacky grammar
- Word choice, e.g. powerful words
- Wordplay, e.g. puns

For each feature, can you remember an example in this book? Look back to find a poem and a quote, and jot them down as examples. Hold a competition with your friends to see who can find the most examples in a limited amount of time.

MY FAVOURITE POEM IS ...

Discussing favourites and backing up your views with quotations and examples is a good way of practising poetry analysis. For example, if you preferred the humour in "Serious Luv" to the subtler tone in "Ice Cream War", why do you think that was?

Pathway into a poem

Reading a new poem can sometimes be scary, especially if it is difficult to understand. Here is a good path to follow – the steps cover your first reading (in blue), the poem's meaning (in yellow), its form (in orange), the vocabulary and other poetic features (in purple), and your decision about whether the poem is successful (in red).

1

2

1 Read the poem through without stopping – don't worry about any bits you don't understand. Jot down your first reactions (e.g., lines that you liked, lines that made you laugh).

2 Read the poem line by line, or sentence by sentence, trying to unpick the full meaning. If you find words difficult, look them up in a dictionary or look at the words around them to see if they give clues to the meaning.

7 Read the poem aloud and clap out the rhythm. What tone does the rhythm give – is it fast or slow? Does it create a happy, light tone, or is it slow and sad? Does the rhythm suddenly stop or change? Can you find a reason why?

7

8 Study the vocabulary in more detail and look for some of the poetic features you have read about in this book. Scan the glossary on pages 59–61 to remind you of poetic features to look for, or use the list on page 51. For any features you find, such as a metaphor, use P.E.E.: note down what it is, copy a quote as evidence, and then give a short explanation of what it adds to the poem.

8

3 Record the main events or images as a numbered set of notes or sketches. Write a précis (one sentence) saying what the whole poem is about.

3

4 Try to find out about the poet and the time in which he or she lived. Can you find anything that seems to link with the meaning of the poem, or that can give you a clue as to the poet's message?

4

5 Consider the form of the poem. Does it have stanzas? If so, how is the information grouped into the stanzas? Do the pauses between stanzas emphasize words in the poem?

5

6 Can you find a rhyme scheme? Has the poet picked meaningful words as rhyming words, or are they there just to rhyme?

6

9 By now you will know the poem well. Have you found any hidden meanings? Think about whether the poet has a message or is trying to get you to think about something or react in a certain way (for example, laugh or feel sad). Your thoughts will answer this question: What are the poem's themes?

9

10 Compare the poem's themes with all that you found in steps 5–8. Do the poem's form and poetic features help to get the message across? Or do they make it blurred and boring? Does the poem use its form and features to affect the reader's thoughts and emotions well? Your thoughts can be used to answer this question: Is the poem successful?

10

Write your own humorous poem

Lots of well-known poets began writing poetry at school. Practice is important, and if you write humorous poetry you can have lots of fun. If you write a poem that makes you laugh, there's a good chance others will laugh at it, too. But remember that humour should never be cruel or embarrassing. Never write humorous poems about people you know – that would be mean and unfair, and other people won't find it funny.

You could base your limerick on this eccentric character.

Write a limerick

A good way to start writing humorous poems is by writing a limerick. Keep it simple by following the form of Edward Lear's limericks, such as this one:

> [line 1] There was an Old Man who said, "Well!
> [line 2] Will nobody answer this bell?
> [line 3] I have pulled day and night,
> [line 4] till my hair has grown white,
> [line 5] But nobody answers this bell!"

There are 8 syllables (3 are stressed) in lines 1, 2, and 5. There are 6 syllables (2 are stressed) in lines 3 and 4. Don't worry about the rhythm too much, but do try to find words that rhyme together for lines 1, 2, and 5, and words that rhyme together for lines 3 and 4. You could begin your limerick with a person and a place name or with something different. If you are stuck for ideas, follow these steps:

1 Think of a person and place name. You can make up a place. Example:
   "There was a young girl of Bagoo"
2 Look in a rhyming dictionary (in a library or on the Internet) for words that rhyme with Bagoo. Choose one for the end of line 2 (e.g., stew, moo, chew, boo, do). It might help you think of an idea for the whole of line 2. Example:
   "Who refused to eat all her stew"
3 Think of two rhyming words for lines 3 and 4. They must link with the idea in line 2. Example:
   "A mouse jumped up
   And licked it all up"
4 You can now finish with a line using the "girl of Bagoo" again. Example:
   "Thank you!" said the girl of Bagoo.

CHECK YOUR RHYTHM

Clap out the Edward Lear limerick to get a feel for the rhythm. When you have finished your limerick, read it aloud and check yours has a similar beat.

Write a nonsense poem

If you want to write a nonsense poem but you don't know where to start, try answering the following questions:

- Theme: what do you want your poem to be about? (Choose a subject you know a lot about or can imagine easily.)
- Viewpoint: will the poem be about your thoughts and experiences or someone else's? (Perhaps start with using your own experiences.)
- Voice: will the voice be your voice or a made-up character's? (You could try using your voice – "I" and "me" – or you as a younger child.)
- Form: will you use stanzas? Will your poem rhyme or be free verse? (Perhaps try the non-stanza form and simple rhyme scheme used in "Sick" on page 31.)

Do a list poem

Your nonsense poem could be a list poem like "Sick". List all the reasons why you cannot do something (e.g. finish your homework or go to the dentist). The reasons could be all the things you have to do first. You could choose silly or nonsense reasons (e.g. you have to cut your toenails, polish your skateboard, give your budgie a bath, take a trip to China on a magic carpet). Alternatively look at a different type of subject, such as silly events at school, embarrassing memories, a sequence of battles between robots, or a journey through a series of fantastical or weird places.

Make up nonce words

To add humour to your list poem, you could make up words. For example, instead of giving your budgie a bath, you could change budgie for a nonsense word that sounds similar, such as "bodgie" or "boggie"; toenails could be "toesnips" or "nailytips". Use made-up adjectives, too, like "slithy" in "Jabberwocky" (page 15), which are two words mixed together.

For ideas on made-up words, look at the word cloud of nonce words opposite. Some of them are Lewis Carroll's, while others are new. Or try creating your own word cloud. It will be a good reference for funny ideas for poems you write now and in the future.

gluggug

gubwit

frumious

wuggy

OUTGRABING

jabberwocky

ZAV

TUGLEY

blorpy

DAX

slithy

BOOJUM

borgrove

SNARK

tulver

vorpal

mimsey

PIMWIT

fendle

blicket

BLUBBUB

HOW TO MAKE A NONCE WORD

Try combining two words to make a new, nonce word.
You can take part of one word and part of another and join
them together, for example:

"busy" plus "working" = borking
"dreary" plus "dark" = dreark
"den" plus "bedroom" = denoom

Put them together and you could include this line in your
list poem:

I'm borking in the dreark of my denoom

Bibliography

The following works provided important sources of information for this book:

Pumpkin Grumpkin, editors John Agard and Grace Nichols (Walker Books, 2011)

Cautionary Verses, Hilaire Belloc (Red Fox, 1995)

The Puffin Book of Nonsense Verse, selected by Quentin Blake (Puffin, 1996)

Alice's Adventures in Wonderland, Lewis Carroll (Penguin Classics, 2006)

Nonsense Verse, Lewis Carroll (Bloomsbury, 2004)

Through the Looking-Glass, and What Alice Found There, Lewis Carroll (Macmillan, 2011)

Completely Crazy Poems, editor John Foster (HarperCollins, 2003)

Fiendishly Funny Poems, editor John Foster (HarperCollins 2004)

A Book of Nonsense, Edward Lear (Everyman's Library, 1992)

The Complete Nonsense of Edward Lear (Faber and Faber, 2001)

How to Avoid Kissing Your Parents in Public, Lindsay MacRae (Puffin, 2000)

A Children's Treasury of Milligan, Spike Milligan (Virgin Books, 2006)

Oh, Terrible Youth, Cristin O'Keefe Aptowicz (Write Bloody Publishing, 2011)

Where the Sidewalk Ends, Shel Silverstein (Particular Books, 2010)

Neighborhood Odes, Gary Soto (Harcourt, 2005)

Grass Sandals: The Travels of Basho, Dawnine Spivak (Atheneum Books for Young Readers, 2009)

Funky Chickens, Benjamin Zephaniah (Puffin, 1997)

Glossary

accent the way words are pronounced or sounded out in a particular region or area of a country

alliteration repetition of sounds at the beginning of words, such as "silver star skylight"

ballad song-like poem

cautionary tale story that serves as a warning about the dangers of behaving in a certain way: e.g. "Little Red Riding Hood" can be seen as a cautionary tale about the dangers of speaking to strangers

conform obey rules or customs

contrasting comparing two different things by putting them close to each other to show off their differences

dramatic effect to be striking and gain the notice of the reader

eccentric person who behaves in an odd or amusing manner

enjambment a sentence or phrase running from one line or stanza to the next, without punctuation to create a pause

epigram short witty poem, often pointing out a human silliness

foot (plural feet) unit of poetry made up of stressed and unstressed syllables

free verse poetry that does not have a regular metre or rhyme

haiku traditional Japanese form of short verse, often with only three lines and 17 syllables

humorous humorous verse is funny or comical, and likely to make the reader smile or laugh

hyperbole ridiculous exaggeration, used for a specific effect, e.g. "I sobbed until my eyes fell out and rolled along the floor" might be written for comic effect

imagery the use of words to form pictures in the reader's mind; imagery can also appeal to senses other than sight, such as touch (e.g. "the soft mud slid between my fingers like an uncooked egg")

irony use of words to suggest a meaning the opposite of their literal meaning

limerick type of humorous verse with five lines, in which the 1st, 2nd, and 5th lines rhyme with each other, and the 3rd and 4th lines rhyme with each other

list poem poem in the form of a long list of items or events

lyricist someone who writes lyrics, or the words of a song

malapropism use of an incorrect word, by mistake, in place of the correct word, which sounds similar. It is often comic, e.g. "This poem is full of ironing" (by "ironing" the writer means "irony")

metaphor comparison between things that are unlike each other without using a word such as "like" or "as"; metaphors can be serious or, as in this case, comic: "My life is bleak – I'm a pickled onion in a screw-top jar"

metre regular pattern of stressed and unstressed syllables in a line of poetry, creating the rhythm of the verse

monologue a speech or one-sided conversation by a poet, character, or other writer or speaker

nonce words words made up for a particular occasion or poem; they are not expected to be used again but may become popular and so become a part of accepted vocabulary

nonsense poetry form of light verse that includes the comic and absurd, and may not make any logical sense or have an obvious meaning

parody mimicry of a style of writing, or ideas, or behaviour; in poetry, parody might mock a poetic form or poet's individual style

pathos anything in a poem that makes us feel pity or sadness

penultimate last but one

phonetically when a word is spelled just as it might be spoken, e.g. "dat" instead of "that"

précis give a short summary of what happens in a story or poem

pun a play on similar-sounding words with various meanings, or on a word that has several meanings, such as: "There once was a man named Cliff / Who lived by the sea ..."

purpose main idea or message that the poet wants to get across to the reader; the purpose in humorous poetry, such as nonsense poetry, may just be to get a laugh

quirky peculiar, or behaving in an unexpected way

quote copy words that have already been written by someone else; they should be put in single or double quotation marks, e.g. The last line repeats the name of the place, "And rapidly rushed about Dutton."

Rastafarian person who follows a Jamaican spiritual movement that worships Emperor Haile Selassie I of Ethiopia (1892–1975)

repressed keeping thoughts and feelings hidden or under control; governed by strict rules

rhyme grouping of words with endings that sound the same (although the endings are not always spelled the same), e.g.: duke, puke; way, weigh

rhythm repeated sound you can hear in spoken poetry, created by patterns of stressed and unstressed syllables

seizure sudden attack, or "fit", brought on by epilepsy or another medical disorder

stanza set of lines within a poem; all the stanzas within a poem may have the same form (e.g. the same rhyme scheme) or they may vary

stressed when words or parts of words sound louder, weightier, or higher pitched when, for example, you read out a phrase or line of poetry

structure form or shape of a poem; for example, the length of the lines, and whether the poem is split into stanzas and, if so, how long they are

syllable word or part of a word that has a separate sound when you say it; for example "limerick" (lim-er-ick) has three syllables

symbol thing that has a meaning beyond what it actually is; e.g. in poetry the season of spring is often a symbol of new beginnings and fresh growth

theme key idea that the poet wants the reader to think about

tongue-twister piece of writing designed to be difficult to say out loud; tongue-twisters often include repeated sounds in words, such as "s" and "sh" in "She sells sea shells on the sea shore"

verse poetry, which is any text that has been written in a specific form with a rhythm and/or pattern of words in mind, and which may also rhyme

vocabulary all the words of a language or dialect, or the words chosen by a poet

vulgar rude and "low class"

Find out more

Research more about Edward Lear

www.nonsenselit.org/Lear/BoN/bon010.html
Edward Lear was a brilliant illustrator as well as a writer of limericks and nonsense poetry. On this site, compare his word portraits with his ink portraits in *A Book of Nonsense*.

Research more about Shel Silverstein

www.shelsilverstein.com/indexsite.html
See Shel Silverstein's website for more of his humorous verse and some illustrations that could inspire your own comic poems.

Research more about nonsense writers

As well as those mentioned in this book, there are many other humorous poets to explore. Try reading some of the poems by these poets and writers:

Hilaire Belloc, 1916–1990, wrote humorous tales about children who misbehaved. Scroll down to read a few at:
allpoetry.com/Hilaire_Belloc
Roald Dahl, 1916–1990, used parody for his funny poems in the collection entitled *Revolting Rhymes* (Puffin, 2009)
Spike Milligan, 1918–2002, wrote lots of silly poems, including "On the Ning Nang Nong", which can be found under "Poems" at:
www.spikemilligan.co.uk
Michael Rosen, 1946–, is a very well-known children's writer and broadcaster. Lots of his humorous verse can be found on his website:
www.michaelrosen.co.uk/poems.html

Research tongue-twister rhymes

www.alphadictionary.com/fun/tongue-twisters/english_tongue_twisters.html
Some poems use repeated sounds so that they are almost impossible to say! Check out a few tongue-twisters on this site, then have a go at writing your own by including as many words with the same initial sound as you can.

To help you write a limerick

www.gigglepoetry.com/poetryclass/limerickcontesthelp.html
This is a useful site for simple step-by-step instructions on how to write
a limerick.

To help you write your own poetry

www.poetry4kids.com/rhymes
For a rhyming dictionary where you can type in a word and ask for a
list of words that contain the same sound.

www.collinsdictionary.com/english-thesaurus
To improve a poem, explore new vocabulary. Type in a word in this
online thesaurus and find others that mean the same thing or have a
similar meaning.

www.wordle.net
Use this website to make a word cloud. A word cloud is a good way
of keeping a record of words you find funny or interesting, and that
might be useful in a poem.

www.poetryfoundation.org/learning/glossary-term/Rhyme
To find out more about the features of poetry, type in a term like
"rhyme" or "rhythm".

Picture acknowledgements
We would like to thank the following for permission to reproduce photographs:
Cover photograph reproduced by permission of ArtFamily/Shutterstock.
Alex Brook Lynn: p. 45; Bridgeman: p. 8 (Look and Learn); Chris Sampson: pp. 16–17;
Corbis: pp. 10 (Heritage Images), 33 (Jeff Albertson); David Morris: p. 27; Dreamstime.com:
pp. 22b (Tjenner), 38 (Dizm), 44 (Notebook), 50 (Camiml), 54 (Urosr); Gary Soto:
p. 39; Getty Images: pp. 6 (Jim Dyson), 11 (Bridgeman), 21 (APIC), 42 (Nicola Tree); Hayley
Madden for the Poetry Society: p. 49b (2011); iStockphoto: pp. 5, 13, 14, 18 (Duncan
Walker), 46; John Tenniel: p. 15; Maureen O'Keefe Aptowicz: p. 40; Online Archive of
California: p. 12 (1910); Shel Silverstein: p. 31 (© 1974, renewed 2002 Evil Eye, LLC);
Shutterstock: pp. 3, 8–9 (Patryk Kosmider), 22t, 23, 24–25, 26, 28, 29, 34, 36, 37, 41, 47, 48,
49t; SuperStock: pp. 19 (Science and Society), 20 (Gerard Lacz Images).

Index